Let The Sh*t Out

Created by Funny Book Art
2020 funny book art

Grab your coloring pencils or crayons.
Sit back. And have fun!
You will love this beautiful coloring book.
It's simply gorgeous!

Each coloring page is located on the right side of
the coloring book, the left side is blank, leaving it
free for you to create beautiful drawings of your
own, journal your thoughts, or simply leave as is.

COLORING TIPS

We have printed the art in single-sided pages. Each image is placed on its own white-backed page to reduce the bleed-through to the next image. If you are using markers, it strongly recommended sliding a piece of cardstock or the thick paper behind the page you are workingon to make sure the ink doesn't stain the next page.

Now Relax and Enjoy your Time

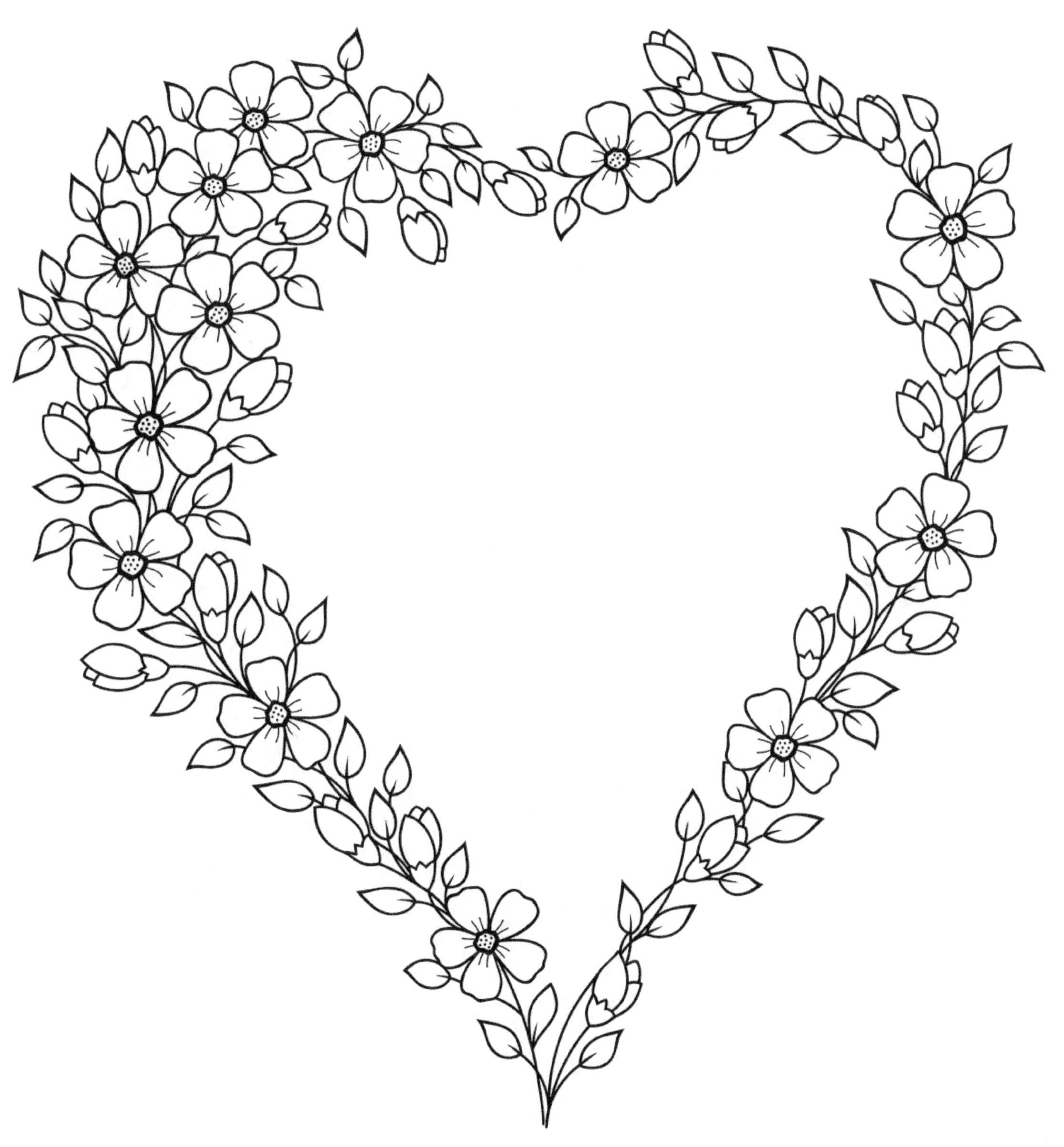

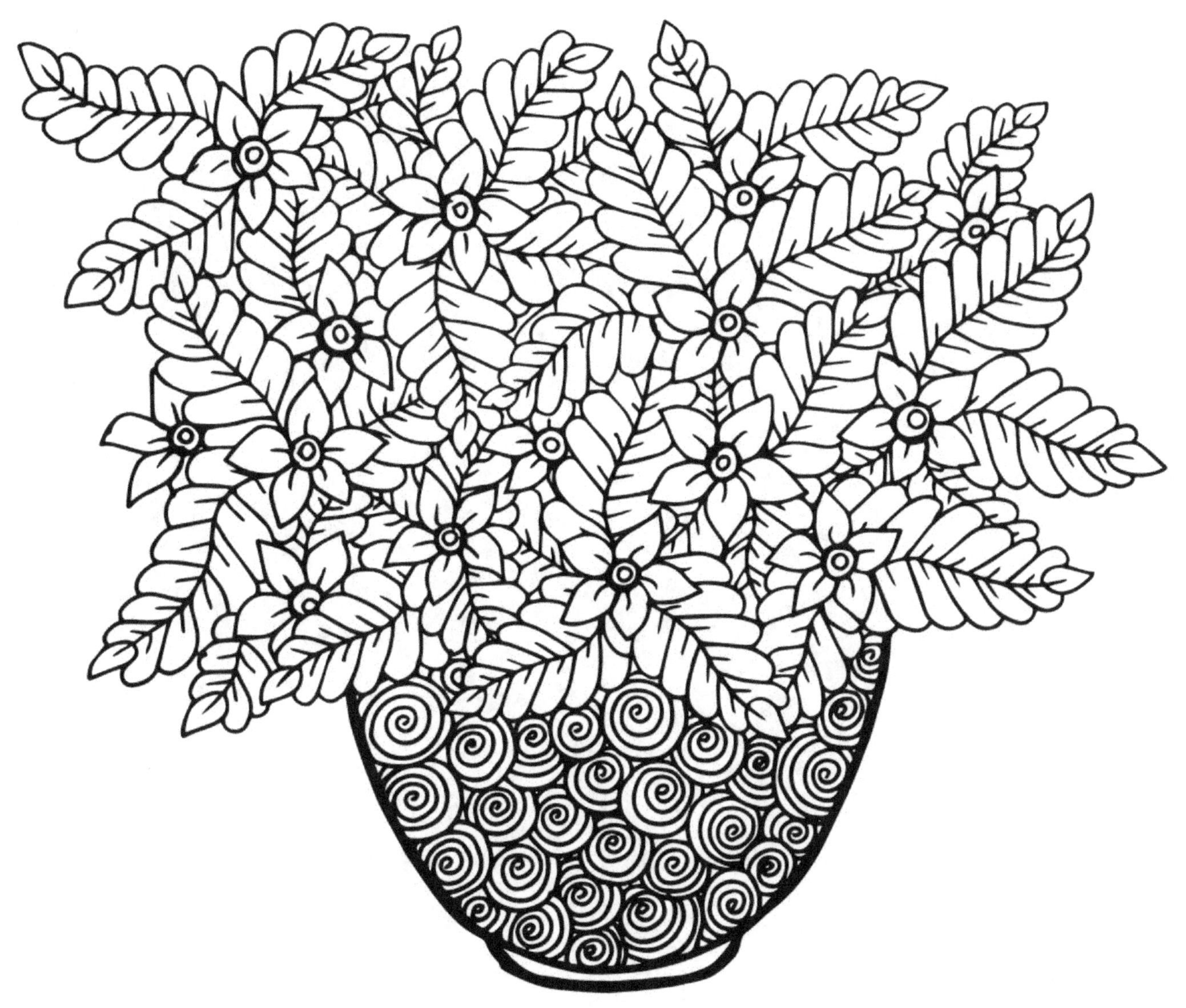